FINISHING LINE PRESS

www.finishinglinepress.com

Dropping Sunrises in a Jar

Poems

by

Melinda Thomsen

Finishing Line Press
Georgetown, Kentucky

Dropping Sunrises in a Jar

For Hunt with all my love

Publisher: Leah Huete de Maines
Editor: Christen Kincaid
Cover Art: Kristiana McKinnon
Author Photo: Hunt McKinnon
Cover Design: Elizabeth Maines McCleavy

Order online: www.finishinglinepress.com
 also available on amazon.com

Author inquiries and mail orders:
Finishing Line Press
PO Box 1626
Georgetown, Kentucky 40324
USA

Contents

I
I'll tell you how the Sun rose—

Within the Rafters 2
Looking at the Sky on April 3rd 3
Dawn at JFK Departure Gate...4
The Zoetrope Sunrise of the Taihang Mountains 6

II
A Ribbon at a time—

Dropping Sunrises in a Jar 8
1. Greenville 10
2. New Year's Day...11
3. Maui 12
4. New York 13
5. Atlantic City 14
6. Prague 15
7. Maine 16
8. Vermont...17
9. Switzerland...18
10. Arizona 19
11. Colorado Springs...20
12. Albany...21
13. The Outer Banks..22
14. Leelanau Peninsula...23
15. On Clear Mornings...24
Sunflowers: Day #83, 17 May 2022.....................................25

III
The Steeples swam in Amethyst—

Sunflower Triage 28
My Skeleton's Pep Talk...29
On Threading Needles with Camels 30
The Sun's Uprising 31

Acknowledgments..32
Notes 33
About the Author 35

I
I'll tell you how the Sun rose—

Within the Rafters

I closed the chicken house door

and looked up at the stars
hanging as if from rafters

when I noticed one
floating across the sky.

Moving five miles per second,
the International Space Station

carries its astronaut cargo,
and from there, they can see

sixteen sunrises every day.

I looked down at my feet
at my home upon this blue marble,

wondering if I could live orbiting
among a daily influx of miracles

and in a constant awe

of what I can't imagine.

Looking at the Sky on April 3rd

As Ukrainians count dead Russian soldiers left behind
In Kyiv and Bacha, our granddaughter turns two months old,

And this evening we watch the International Space Station fly over
Our neighborhood from the northwest to southwest in four minutes.

The station appears as a bright flashlight gliding through the night
Until its solar panels no longer reflect the sun, and it shrinks from sight.

On board, astronauts from NASA, the European Space Agency,
And Roscosmos work together and when they pass by, I wave,

I want to believe the ring on my finger reflects a bit of streetlight
That they might see my flashing, signaling that someone lives

Here, and she hasn't blown herself up yet in a blaze of hubris.
I look skyward to remind every star willing itself to glow; *we are here.*

Dawn at JFK Departure Gate

A pigeon nesting in the eves
coos as the sun rises,
and a plane leaves.

Dawn casts its runways
of light through twenty
foot tall windows,

and sparrows fly low
through the terminal
above the masked

passengers at the gates.
Here we sit corralled
and hushed, unaware

of all the wax
and feathers it takes
to fly towards the sun.

At home, I watch doves
outstretch their wings
and ascend upwards for yards

as if nothing could happen,
as if no hawk ever circles
above our house,

or no car could ever suck
them under its chassis
and leave them fluttering

awkwardly by the side
of the road. Unlike them,
I head into safety or peril

trailing a hundred worries.
I embark for six months
across the Atlantic,

as the anti-Icarus
who has planned her escape
to survive the flight.

The Zoetrope Sunrise of the Taihang Mountains

Waking in a sleeper car, bunked
with three strangers, I raise the shade

to watch the sunrise, a pale peach glow,
among the snoring. Cornfields stretch

beneath gauzy clouds as our train enters
a tunnel and metal sounds reflect

off its stone interior. As we exit,
the ochre sky lightens, then another

tunnel and again a waterfall of noise.
Now, the sun glows behind mountain

peaks, and mist rests in the Taihang
valley of lush shrubbery when a tunnel

eclipses that view. The train
travels through tunnel after tunnel,

but between glimpses, the sun rises.
and we emerge into a village

with streams edging the foothills
framed with cornfields and box houses.

A man feeds his donkey.
The child in our cabin coughs.

For the Chinese, *the road over
Taihang* means *the frustrations of life.*

Where the sun rises through slits,
this zoetrope carries me home,

or some place where I can untangle
myself through flashes of beauty.

I had to get out through stillness;
until bit by bit, the womb opened.

II
A Ribbon at a time—

Dropping Sunrises in a Jar

When daybreak edged the earth,
        I would roll over—unlike the birds.
It was as if we lived in separate jars.
        Wrens whistle and chirp about flames
blooming into a ball at sunrise
        then hush with the sun's full burning.

I used to sleep through the daily burning
        for I didn't care much how the earth
rotated itself into another sunrise.
        But years later, I wondered why birds
got so excited about a horizon in flames.
        So much time, I've spent within a jar.

The birds, too, live in a sort of jar,
        but they focus outward and seem to burn
with a gratitude that fans their inner flame.
        See pelicans fly above the earth?
They dip and lift until the idea of *bird*
        becomes a winged embrace at sunrise.

When I traveled, I watched every sunrise
        to see night leave its door to morning ajar,
and in its wake, I heard the calls from birds.
        Each place began with its horizon burning,
though, and I worry our Goldilocks earth
        is ending. We choose to go in flames,

or up in smoke like a moth drawn to a flame
        when *just right* gets *too hot*, but each sunrise
still unleashes warbling tenors upon the earth.
        For we don't see birds flying into bell jars
or coal mines, do we? While forests burn
        in the west, in the east, squirrels and birds

gear up for hurricanes. Notice how *birds*
        of a feather fly from floods and flames?
Instead, I wake to the sky's daily burning
        in these—my sunset—years to collect sunrises.
One by one, I drop them in a jar
        like candies gathered from my forgiving earth.

But this burning keeps flushing out the birds,
           who welcome the earth as if an old flame
and add their sunrise songs to its tip jar.

1. Greenville

First come the crows, sparrows, and clerks,
as the donut makers carry on,
and the sun burns at the horizon,
trailing its pink and ochre lacework.

Starlings swoop and perch as a display
of a hundred. What do they know of sun?
What limited hues define their vision?
Our yellow dwarf star draws in this new day

and warms me by degrees. Our daily bond
with earth ends at sunset when a glass of wine
lights a flame in my eyes. With one quick

toast, I'll send the sun back into the ground.
I feel birds tugging on my heart like twine,
but I'm a flame holding to her wick.

2. New Year's Day

I'm only a flame holding to her wick,
as the decade enters streamed in flutes
of clouds. Commuters take their routes
across bridges edged with lamps clicking

off pearly lights. The horizon behind
a building glows burnt orange as more
cars hum by and dawn arrives pouring
peach and amber in the sky. Aligned

on power lines, starlings keep their rows,
facing sunward and waiting. Towards the east
behind some trees, the sun's a growing flare

shaping into a sword, and birds crow
when the sun rises like a flaming beast
and earth ushers in its *power star.*

3. Maui

When earth ushers in its *power star,*
my friend says her sunrise arrives
with chattering mynas which drive
her crazy. Next, a deep mauve appears

in the horizon almost the same
way as here. Photos of a palm tree
sweeping an arc across the sky, and three
tourists, bright as *Skittles,* arrive to claim

their spots on the beach. I smell the saline
Pacific breezes, but here in the east, currents
control the Atlantic's warming tidal wars,

which heave back and forth into hurricanes.
While NASA searches for suitable planets,
Goldilocks considers moving to Mars.

4. New York

As Goldilocks considers moving to Mars,
some heavy metal-colored clouds hang low
and rose contrails drift near the Triboro
Bridge. At dawn, squawking gulls glide far

above while I lean on the railing of iron bars.
The birds get so excited. Why can't I let go
with joy at rising suns like sparrows?
They chirp in maple trees with a repertoire

that ascends. The pigeons unite in an arc
across the striped dawn's sky crisscrossed
with ocher, rust, and beige. Rubies glow

upon the bridge's pylons and dot the dark.
The sun arrives in the finale to toss
its molten light and speckle the surf below.

5. Atlantic City

Molten light speckles the surf below,
and above me Trump's neon Taj Mahal—
this was before he wanted to *build a wall.*
That day a red sun rose streaming yellow

and pink ribbons lightly touching the sea.
The greenish gold streams of dawn then peeled
away to a reddish orange which almost revealed
the hope of another day as the sun simply

appeared, framed in scarlet and then evolved
into gold flecks stretching to the shore,
and waves clattered like coins before dissolving.

The day arrived, and I went back indoors,
pulling damask drapes on all involved.
The brass handle flashed at my door.

6. Prague

The polished handle flashes at the door
when light reaches the Diplomat Hotel.
The sun's a burning coin whose strength swells
and glows above the trees. Nearby, four

trams enter Dejvicka Station as scores
of commuters descend the Métro's stairwells.
Here, no chatty pigeons or sparrows foretell
the dawn—just traffic, sounding more and more

like an orchestra of cars humming
and busses braking with squeals that hiss.
Even a fountain flares its beating drums.

While tourists like me sleep, the Czechs insist
on construction with cranes that jerk and thrum
with a screeching that lifts, not even mist.

7. Maine

With a screeching that lifts, not even mist,
the warblers, nuthatches, and oven birds
are dawn's harbingers that wake and lure
me from bed. The late risers consist

of crows cawing and sounding rather pissed.
Across the way, the sun arrives mirrored
in the pond, and its flaming self appears
between the oaks. A chipmunk clucks amidst

a motley bird chorus raising hell
with *whitchity wheeps* and *fee bees* pouring
from trees. These winged critters send spells

full throttle to wake the entire forest.
Daylight inches into the woodland floor
while waves of leaves rattle and twist.

8. Vermont

While waves of leaves rattle and twist,
four crows take off across the parking lot.
They joust and squawk with wings flared out.
One hops from grass to curb as if bewitched

by some ancient avian drumming beat
that's lost on me. At six, a fiery dot
appears above this valley with rays wrought
in fog. It morphs into a cross that meets

the lawn and blossoms into an orange light
reflecting off the cars and trucks. The sun
is now over the mountain, and burns white

in the sky. My pen dribbles what occurs
on the page as I wonder why I am undone
by birds flying like commas into conifers.

9. Switzerland

The birds fly like commas into conifers
when winter's sun appears as a cornstalk
that blooms and sprays its rays. Contrails chalk
the blackboard sky in an easterly swirl

and silver flecks from jets' bellies — an ocean
where the sun embarks from its mountain dock
into the sky's palm with grayish dark
fingers, and its flaming hurts my vision.

The belfries in the valley welcome the year.
A magpie hops from bare branch to conifer,
and clouds burn gold, but more blotches smear

my sight as sunlight runs from snow to trees.
I turn my gaze into the shadows of firs
where only darkness stops tracks like these.

10. Arizona

Only darkness stops the sound tracks of these
noisy birds when the sun remains bound
behind the Catalinas, and sky appears gowned
and glowing. An intro by canyon towhees

leads to ditties by kinglets and chickadees,
next vireos trill their songs. The waking ground
offers an a cappella riff in varying rounds
of chortles, even a waxwing joins the glee!

Suddenly, a quail coughs and a dove lands
on a spindly branch, letting her tail feathers tap
a beat like a brush—a drummer for their band.

Doves perching on wires send coos into the world.
When notes of their coda begin, I almost clap
but hold my breath. The sun emerges unfurled.

11. Colorado Springs

In a breath, the sun emerges unfurled
behind the hangar, and the sky turns gold.
It burns like an ore, as nearby grasses roll
in a breeze, and rows of sunflowers twirl

and flex. The Queen Anne's lace slowly maps
the sun's route west. A magpie somewhere
near the playing field squawks. Dawn appears
in shades of granite wearing a mica cap.

Let me put on the sky's sapphire chains
and earth's necklace of headlights from the cars
winding to Denver in their jeweled train.

When headlamps dim, sunshine shoots like stars
off the cargo bays of arriving planes,
and daybreak shows its wealth by reaching far.

12. Albany

Daybreak shows its wealth by reaching far
between office buildings covered by windows
with some still lit. I look down below
where crosswalks and lights alert the cars.

Bruegger's Bagel beams its neon red
into the dawn. Over the river, low
and dark, a tower's crimson pulsing throws
its beams across the sky in threads.

As the lapis night recedes, it's replaced
by a citrine dawn with a commuter train firing
off its whistle at every crossing place.

The earth turns more, so I return my keys
and check out, but as the sun gets higher
finches wake cheeping in distant trees.

13. The Outer Banks

Finches wake cheeping in distant trees,
but, here, a haze hovers above the ocean.
Tides break, as pelicans lift on breezes.
Three gulls tarry by the shore. The sun

appears under gauzy clouds then sinks
behind its whitish bandages into surf.
From the beach, we hold warm drinks
and scan the sky, dunes, and dying turf

when the sun appears, and gunmetal
waves roll in another muted thunder,
gathering up lost shells or unsettled

ones. Morning barrels down, and our star
at the edge of the world burns it asunder.
Another day opens this kind of jar.

14. Leelanau Peninsula

Another day opens this kind of jar
with a sun's fiery arms edging dawn
of Grand Traverse Bay whose horizon
streaks peach then dusty gold; crickets spar.

The sun slowly lifts in the sky's palm
where gulls trail silhouettes on a blue
sky like scattered checks. We're all through.
The sun, a copper eye, delves the calm

morning. Fires seem to pulse the waves.
In a minute, the eye morphs into a hot coal
shooting rays westward as if depraved.

Our Promethean earth rolls forward to work,
but we lapse and neglect our basic role
to save the crows, sparrows and clerks.

15. On Clear Mornings

First come the crows, sparrows and clerks,
but I'm more the flame holding to her wick,
as the earth ushers in our power star,
and Goldilocks considers moving to Mars.

See molten light speckling surf and shore
where polished handles flash from doors?
There's screeching that lifts, not even mist,
and waves of leaves start to rattle and twist.

While birds fly like commas into conifers,
only darkness stops tracks like these.
In a breath, the sun emerges unfurled,

and daybreak displays its wealth by reaching far,
so finches start cheeping in distant trees.
Another day opens this kind of jar.

Sunflowers: Day #83, 17 May 2022
Inspired by Nikola Yurtsaba's photo

Today, I pressed
sunflower seeds into

potting soil, placed their tray
under a grow light, and waited.

In a month, I'll transplant them outside
to stretch into stalks for their one-eyed

heads. On Twitter, a Ukrainian writer wears
combat boots covered with sunflowers and skulls,

but those skulls fade behind the sunflowers,
which draw death into themselves. So, no wonder

sunflowers in the Ukraine flourish in fields
where people have died. Their acres of sunflowers

compose 70 to 80% of all sunflower oil exports, and
after Chernobyl, sunflowers were sown to extract

radioactive metals from the soil into their stems
and leaves. Over 4000 years ago, Native Americans

harvested these wide-eyed beauties, and mine
droop every fall from faces bearing their drying

rug of seeds. With a twist, I release each
black arrowhead containing the world's

future yellow, and let it drop
into my cupped palm.

III
The Steeples swam in Amethyst—

Sunflower Triage

I found a sunflower laying
sideways in the cucumber bed,
unearthed with its roots in tact.

Placed in a cup, it leaned
its broken self on a chopstick
for balance to grow upwards.

Think of your own plot of earth
where your new roots finger
outward to pull in a nutrient, or two.

That is terror. I only need a sip
of earth water, but a thimble full
is so scant. I want more than enough.

As I placed flowers in soil
and sunlight, a wren chortled
at the breeze or transplants, or whoever

would listen. After several weeks,
all sunflowers stood without a cane
or crutch, erect in newly dug furrows.

Although dwarfed, they stretched
into the sky and turned sunward
until their faces spread like saucers.

Five loaves of bread and two fish
fed 5000, like water droplets
that sustain one helianthus.

My Skeleton's Pep Talk

I do my best to hold you up.
Even all those years you heard,
Don't hunch over so.

*Stand up straight. Throw your
shoulders back.* As if posture
depends only on calcium

rich bones and attitude.
I can't make every little
girl stand ballerina straight.

So much sadness gets in the way.

Let's forget about roses
stooped over in dry vases.

Look at how birds stand
with backs arched and proudly
focus on being a bird.

Hear the wren each morning
using its skeletal gift
at full throttle?

It's not my doing alone.
One day, you'll shape yourself
into the bird
           your soul holds.

On Threading Needles with Camels

"It is easier for a camel to go through the eye of a needle than for a rich man to enter the kingdom of God." Matthew 19:21-24

My husband wears jeweler's glasses to thread needles
As he patches clothes. When I see him sewing, I see camels.

If I took a lock of camel hair and threaded it into a needle,
Camels go through. If I held an entire camel with some pulley system

And heaved its 600 plus pounds upward, turning it to fit
Through a two-story opening in a needle welded from steel,

Would St. Peter throw open heaven for us all?
One strand of camel's hair carries its DNA, but leaves its weight,

Speed, and height behind. If I moistened a lock of camel hair
With my saliva, twisted it, and thread the needle, would we both

Go to heaven? If I pulled out of myself one bit of inner *camel*—
The part that lopes through deserts, shuttling tourists without bitching—

Would I be more decent? Perhaps, I overthink proverbs,
But I love how camels chew, spit, and walk out of sunrises.

The Sun's Uprising

The Sun responds to John Donne's "The Sun Rising"

> *Busy old fool, unruly,* Donne,
>   you're such a pain;
> pull those east-facing drapes to greet the sun.
> My job's to brighten the day, so why complain?
>   Even school kids are up and gone.
>   The snails and ants have faster gaits
>   than you, for it's already an hour past dawn!
>   God knows your Sunday's sermon cannot wait,
> so please wake up your mistress for me, as well,
> and I will resume my daily carousel.

>   Really? You prefer to roll in bed,
>   scorning my rays
> to bask in your sweetie's shining eyes, instead?
> Why not enjoy this morning's full display
>   of a fuchsia defined horizon
>   and swirling flocks of trilling starlings?
>   The earth doesn't slow to a cedar resin's
>   pace at your flat, or refrain from its whirling.
> It's Copernicus's law we abide by.
> Excuse me, but you've got the wrong bad guy.

>   Okay, I see how she's your moon,
>   and I'm a pest.
> This afternoon's eclipse should change your tune
> and usher in some darkness to your nest.
>   This spinning system can't ignore
>   its duty, so don't risk your health
>   or sanity with chatter calling for
>   more sex. Rather, enjoy my prince's wealth
> of dew tipped roses with your dearest friend
> and let love blossom until the stars descend.

ACKNOWLEDGMENTS

The author would like to thank the editors of the following books or journals who first published these poems.

Big City Lit—"8. Vermont;" "9. Switzerland"
Comstock Review—"10. Arizona"
Hermit Feathers Review—"1. Greenville"
Kakalak 2023 Anthology of Poets and Artists—"Dropping Sunrises in a Jar"
The Paddock Review—"Dawn at JFK Departure Gate"
Pinesong Awards Anthology—"The Sun's Uprising"
Poetry in Performance: 51—"Dawn at JFK Departure Gate"
The Same—"4. New York "New York;" "5. Atlantic City;" 6. Prague;" "7. Maine"
What Rough Beast—"Sunflower Triage"

Special Thanks

I would like to acknowledge my friends and family who not only watched sunrises with me but offered loving encouragement as I tried to capture each sunrise on paper. First of all, I want to thank my writing group, Elizabeth J. Coleman and Kate Fetherston, who have spent many hours with these poems over the past seven years. They have offered invaluable advice to bring these pieces into form. I am deeply indebted to my North Carolina friends like Jeanne Julian, Margaret Tau, Regina YC Garcia, Caren Stuart, Kelly Jones, Debbie Metcalf, Kristie Williams, and Celestine Davis, who have been my most enthusiastic cheerleaders! Finally, I am indebted to my family, Larry, Kanako, and Kenneth Thomsen, Kristiana McKinnon, Wilder Rose Hardee, Duncan Hardee, and my husband Hunt, who is my true poem.

NOTES

#318, "I'll tell you how the Sun rose—"
Sections named after the first three lines of Emily Dickinson's poem in *The Complete Poems of Emily Dickinson*, edited by Thomas H. Johnson, Little Brown, 1960, p.150.

"The Zoetrope Sunrise of the Taihang Mountains"
First published as "Taihang Mountains, Southeast of Beijing" in *Armature*, Hermit Feathers Press, 2021.

"10. Arizona"
Special Merit Winner for the Comstock Review's Muriel Craft Bailey Award 2019.

"14. Leelanau Peninsula"
Formally "Grand Traverse Bay 6:30 a.m." – Featured poem in the artist Carole Steinberg Berk's painting exhibit 13 Ways of Looking at a Leelanau Sunrise at Martha's in Sutton Bay, Michigan in October 2012.

"Sunflowers: Day #83, 17 May 2022"
Nikola Yurtsaba, @NYurtsaba Tweet, posted at 6:47 AM on May 17, 2022. https://twitter.com/NYurtsaba/status/1526514865224966145?s=20

"On Threading Needles with Camels"
A semi-finalist for both the North Carolina Writers' Network's Randall Jarrell Poetry Prize in 2021 and The North Carolina Literary Review's Applewhite Poetry Contest in 2020.

"The Sun's Uprising"
This poem is the Sun's response to "The Sun Rising" poem by John Donne where the Sun mimics Donne's first line. The stanzas mirror Donne's concerns, rhyme scheme, and meter. It won Second Place in the Joanna Catherine Scott Award in the 2020 North Carolina Poetry Society Contest.

Melinda Thomsen lives in Greenville, North Carolina with her husband Hunt McKinnon, two cats, and one chicken. A graduate of Mount Holyoke College, she holds an MA in English from The City College of New York, MFA in Writing from Vermont College of Fine Arts, and works as the Writing Center Coordinator at John Paul II Catholic High School in Greenville. Her full length collection *Armature* from Hermit Feathers Press (2021) was a finalist for the 2022 Eric Hoffer da Vinci Eye award and an honorable mention in the 2019 Lena Shull Poetry Contest from North Carolina Poetry Society. Her books *Field Rations* (2011) and *Naming Rights* (2007) are also from Finishing Line Press, and her latest poems can be found in *Salamander Magazine*, *Artemis Journal*, *THEMA*, *The Ekphrastic Review*, *Poetry Miscellany*, *The New York Quarterly*, and *Poetry Quarterly*, among others. Her poems have won many awards, including a 2023 Randall Jarrell Poetry Contest Honorable Mention, 2019 Pushcart Nominee from *The Comstock Review*, and a Semi-Finalist in the 2004 "Discovery" / *The Nation* poetry contest. She's an advisory editor for *Tar River Poetry*.

www.ingramcontent.com/pod-product-compliance
Lightning Source LLC
Chambersburg PA
CBHW020224090426
42734CB00008B/1210